STORY/TIME

THE TONI MORRISON LECTURE SERIES

cosponsored by Princeton University Center for African
American Studies and Princeton University Press

STORY/TIME

The Life of an Idea

BILL T. JONES

Princeton University Press

Princeton and Oxford

Published by Princeton University Press, 41 William Street, Princeton, New Jersey 08540
In the United Kingdom: Princeton University Press, 6 Oxford Street, Woodstock,
    Oxfordshire OX20 1TW

press.princeton.edu

Jacket photograph © Timothy Greenfield-Sanders. All rights reserved.
Photos on pages 9, 10, 13, 99, 100, and 106 courtesy of Bjorn G. Amelan.
Photo on page 18 courtesy of Sameer A. Khan / Fotobuddy.
Photos on pages 81, 82, 84, 85, and 94–96 courtesy of Gene Pittman for Walker Art Center,
    Minneapolis.
Photos on pages 83 and 86–93 courtesy of Paul B. Goode, 2012, performance photos for
    New York Live Arts.
Story on p. 55 courtesy of Daniel Ladinsky, p. 123 in *The Gift: Poems by Hafiz*. Penguin, 1999.
Library of Congress Cataloging-in-Publication Data

Jones, Bill T.
Story/Time : the Life of an Idea / Bill T. Jones.
pages cm. -- (The Toni Morrison Lecture Series)
ISBN 978-0-691-16270-6 (hardcover : acid-free paper) 1. Literature, Experimental. I.
    Title.
PS3610.O617S76 2014
814'.6--dc23
            2013050410

British Library Cataloging-in-Publication Data is available

This book is published with the generous support of the Center for African American
    Studies at Princeton University

This book has been composed in Verdigris and Syntax

Printed on acid-free paper. ∞
Printed in China

10 9 8 7 6 5 4 3 2 1

CONTENTS

ACKNOWLEDGMENTS

I wish to thank Princeton University President Shirley M. Tilghman; Professor Eddie Glaude, Chair of the Center for African American Studies; Professor Daphne Brooks and the Toni Morrison Lectures Selection Committee; Chuck Myers and Fred Appel of Princeton University Press; and all the staff, faculty, students, and members of the public who made my Toni Morrison Lectures a memorable and stimulating experience. I also wish to thank Toni Morrison, the creator of an inspiring body of work and so vivid as a woman and as a friend.

The April 2012 public performance at Princeton in connection with my Toni Morrison Lectures was a solo variation on *Story/Time*, a Bill T. Jones/Arnie Zane Dance Company work premiered in January 2012 at Montclair State University's Peak Performances series. *Story/Time* was co-commissioned by Peak Performances at Montclair State University and the Walker Art Center. The piece was produced by New York Live Arts and developed in residence at Arizona State University Gammage Auditorium, Bard College, Alexander Kasser Theater at Montclair State University, University of Virginia, and the Walker Art Center. I would like to express gratitude to Jedediah Wheeler of Peak Performances at Montclair State University for his ongoing support of my work over the years.

The creation of new work by the Bill T. Jones/Arnie Zane Dance Company is made possible by the Company's Partners in Creation: Ellen Poss, Jane Bovingdon Semel and Terry Semel, Anne Delany, Stephen and Ruth Hendel, Eleanor Friedman and Jonathan Cohen, and Sandra Eskin. The work is also funded in part by the New England Foundation for the Arts' National Dance Project, with lead funding from the Doris Duke Charitable Foundation and additional funding from the Andrew W.

Mellon Foundation and the Boeing Company Charitable Trust.

Integral to the performance at Princeton were the contributions of composer Ted Coffey, sound designer Sam Crawford, and artist Bjorn Amelan. I also wish to express my appreciation to Thelma Golden, Director of the Studio Museum in Harlem; Laura Kuhn, Director of The John Cage Trust; and writer and music critic John Rockwell for agreeing to take part in a series of very helpful prelecture conversations with me. I also thank educator Simon Dove, former director of the Arizona State University School of Dance in the Herberger Institute for Design and the Arts. The lectures at Princeton were produced with the assistance of the staff of New York Live Arts and the Bill T. Jones/Arnie Zane Dance Company, including Janet Wong, Bob Bursey, Kyle Maude, Laura Bickford, Victoria Michelotti, Nicholas Lazzaro, and Andrew Dinwiddie. This book would not be possible without the loving and tireless efforts of Bjorn Amelan.

Story/Time is a meditation on John Cage's *Indeterminacy*, a 1958 work in which John Cage read ninety stories, each one minute long. *Indeterminacy*, for me, is both a comfort and a provocation. It encapsulates pillars of Cage's thoughts regarding time, content, intention, non-intention, the role of chance, and the insights of Buddhist philosophy within the poetry of performance. Engaging with this seminal work allowed me to examine and interrogate a system of thought and practice grounded in ideas held by many—myself included—striving to understand how Eastern thought, liberation philosophy, and art could be used to redefine reality for both the maker and his or her audience.

The object you are holding in your hands is conflicted. It is a performance yearning to be a document, a book. It is the printed artifact of the three Toni Morrison Lectures I was invited by the Center for African American Studies to deliver at Richardson Auditorium and McCosh Hall at Princeton University. These spaces are intimate, with 880 and 370 seats, respectively. My inclination in all performances is to take into consideration the physical spaces themselves. This personalizes each performance and underlines a basic assumption I have that no time-based event can be separated from the when and where it is done.

The lecture halls never quite became a theater; still they were arenas where many voices—my own being one of them—collided, protested, remembered, confessed, and defied each other. The lecture halls became echo chambers complete with a sound installation that transformed and theatricalized the voices of which the text is composed. The purpose of this was to create an experience aimed at demonstrating as opposed to describing a manner of thinking, a way of being.

This object, this book, is an effort desiring to communicate directly and still it remains indeterminate in much the same way the dances I create for the stage do. These talks were described as a thought journey in pursuit of "the life of an idea." It is the record of a needy, angry, and confused man. The need is for a tradition, an intellectual home. The anger is generated from an ever-maturing realization that I never truly had an intellectual home and never will.

This conflicted document exists because of a process very much like the one I subjected John Cage to by reducing him to a strict set of principles and then shaping this reduction into an effigy that is to be pushed and pulled, interrogated and worshipped.

The research that lead me to fashion the John Cage effigy was informed among other things by conversations I had with three generous individuals: historian and critic John Rockwell; Laura Kuhn, Director of the John Cage Trust; and Thelma Golden, Director of the Studio Museum in Harlem. I am indebted to all three of them. These conversations became the opportunity to use the Cage effigy as a troubling compass, a way through "the forest of signs": race, identity, aesthetic influences, tradition, spirituality, memory, beauty, intention, and non-intention.

My editor has set himself the task of retrieving a recognizable voice and a narrative from the echo chamber/"forest of signs"— my voice. I, on the other hand, stay committed to a conundrum— this conflicted object as an artifact of "an experimental action," the value of which is less its originality than its authenticity, less a well-wrought argument than an indeterminate performance.

The elements in this book are my thoughts, quotations from others, short stories I have written, and photos. Both quotes and stories are flora and fauna in the forest of signs.

The photographs, sometimes records of actual performances, sometimes purposefully ambiguous signs, act as players amid the landscape of the text. The different font types, consciously mimicking Cage, are intended to have different weights, colors, and distances from the observer/reader/audience, recalling Sam Crawford's sound design in the actual lecture halls.

The look and feel of this book, which owe so much to Director of Design Maria Lindenfeldar and Designer Karl Spurzem, are an invitation to play; to take it as a whole or piecemeal; to reorder it if you will.

The lectures had three parts: *Past Time*, *Story/Time*, and *With Time*.

Past Time and *With Time* were self-consciously about ideas, often confessional and designed for the ear, as I am not a scholar, academic, or researcher, but rather a maker of live performances and a performer. The middle section, *Story/Time*, is a compendium of sixty short narratives, each designed to be read aloud in a one-minute time-frame. Here is a poker-faced plundering of Cage's *Indeterminacy*, allowing me to be by turns direct, elusive, ironic, sincere, and/or metaphorical.

This section was the most performative of all three events, complete with lighting by Laura Bickford, Sam Crawford's sound design, a musical composition by Ted Coffey, and Bjorn Amelan's ever-morphing drawings on a blackboard.

In a conversation with Thelma Golden, she called me out on the unacknowledged anxiety I have in embracing John Cage as an influence. The restating of his *Indeterminacy* in *Story/Time* and as the spirit informing this book is a blatant and defiant retort:

Yes, Cage is my father, but his strategy becomes stranger still because of the divergence and contrast in our personalities; expression of the idea of *Indeterminacy*; and how, where, when, and for whom it is presented. This is for me the latest chapter in the life of an idea!

STORY/TIME

What is the nature of an experimental action? It is simply an action the outcome of which is unforeseen.

—John Cage, *Silence*

To take another man's idea, to develop it, expand it, to impose on its logic a super-logic; this does imply an element of criticism.

—Morton Feldman, "Boola Boola," an essay from *Give My Regards to Eighth Street*

The new confuses the old. Sometimes they enhance each other, sometimes they do just the opposite. Manet, for instance, because of "the new" no longer looks so unfinished.

—Morton Feldman

The first time I heard or saw John Cage was in 1972 at SUNY Binghamton. How I—a theater/dance major—happened to be present there in the Student Commons of the brand-new "College in the Woods" is a mystery to me forty years later.

I remember the long table at which John Cage sat with, I believe, David Tudor and several other musicians behind a bank of microphones, reel-to-reel tape machines, amplifiers, a profusion of wires, and perhaps a traditional instrument or two. To the left of this table was a rowboat standing on its end. Next to it was a young woman in sweater and blue jeans. The room had been specially wired for sound with some speakers, most of them up near the ceiling. As I remember, the sounds were of nature in constant interactive flux with electronic drones, whirring, whines, tweets, and scraping metallic noise. At one point one of the musicians ran a microphone round the contours of the boat as he later did around the mildly embarrassed woman. During the evening it was explained that the microphone was picking up frequencies bouncing off the boat and woman that fed back into the system. This caused a shift in pitch, timbre, and volume in the soundscape all around us as we stood or sat on the floor, chairs, and couches of this common room.

Though my focus was on theater and athletics, I had already developed the habit of attending lectures and screenings in the Cinema Department and was discussing the performance with one of the young instructors, a filmmaker. He said that most striking for him was that amid all the avant-garde soundscaping there were birdcalls where one expected to find them—up near the ceiling!

Two impressions stayed with me after the performance: the first was just how bewildering the event had been, and the second was a realization that I had been bored and yet could not stop thinking about the event for days after. The event taught me that boredom is not a problem in and of itself.

I start with this memory because that night proved to be a sort of second birth, or coming into consciousness, of the world of ideas or what one might call a tradition of artistic discourse. I cannot say I was really part of this tradition at the time. I was more like a newcomer, hearing the din and spirited exchanges of a heated debate from an anteroom.

At that time SUNY Binghamton's Cinema Department was arguably one of the best in the country for experimental cinema.

Bill T. Jones, 1972. Courtesy of Binghamton University. Photo by Evangelos Dousmanis.

And in this department I was given an essential concept: art is an exercise in perception. This exercise of John Cage was probably the most troubling and powerful example of this notion.

Though I had come to the university with every notion of being an actor and discovered dance along the way, that night made it possible for me to realize that performance as art making would be a means by which I could validate my place in the world. Amid all the hurly-burly of the counterculture, with its mind-expanding drugs, music, and various other roads to transcendence, I felt uneasy. Did I experience this unease because of my race? My sexuality? Was it just being young during the Cold War? For whatever reason, I needed a way to understand how to live in this world—and art making, performance, became that.

In Cage, who after that performance represented for me a sophisticated "remove" of imagination/invention over reality, I could take shelter from the social structure I was born into. This remove restated the siren song of the '60s counterculture's declarations:

This is a time of transformation! You are not your body! You are not this thing that has a meaning beyond your control, inscrutable in its past and terrifying in its future! You will be free if you declare yourself free! The only cost of this freedom is to cut yourself off from the "straight" world and any investments, influences, or entanglement it demands!

(At that time, the word "straight"—like so many other terms of common use today—was in flux.)

Earlier I referred to a tradition of artistic discourse because it expands the notion of art making beyond the commonly held views of it as the individual pursuit of masterpieces and the glory/immortality they are supposed to bestow. Discourse expands art practice into something broader, more democratic—a participation in the world of ideas.

The question is: Is my thought changing? It is and it isn't. One evening after dinner I was telling friends that I was now concerned with improving the world. One of them said: "I thought you always were." I then explained that I believe—and am acting upon—Marshall McLuhan's statement that we have through electronic technology produced an extension of our brains to the world formerly outside of us. To me that means that the disciplines, gradual and sudden (principally Oriental), formerly practiced by individuals to pacify their minds, bringing them into accord with ultimate reality, must now be practiced socially—that is, not just inside our heads, but outside of them, in the world, where our central nervous system effectively now is.

John Cage, foreword to *A Year from Monday: New Lectures and Writings* (1963)

I use the term "discourse" in the way we have grown accustomed to describing certain social phenomena as movements. We speak of the Labor Movement, the Civil Rights Movement, the Environmental Movement, the Countercultural Movement, the Women's Movement, the LGBT Movement.

Movement, as its name implies, is a phenomenon that progresses, has a direction, a past and a future. It is the practice of a group; there is no movement of one. In the context of art history, modernism is a movement with its foundation myth, its architects, its factions, its orthodoxies, and—as postmodern performer/choreographer Steve Paxton once told me—its research branch that another time would have called its avant-garde.

Discourse is sometimes defined as "a written or spoken communication or debate" and as "a formal discussion of a topic in speech or writing," and in the context of art, as I understand it, as practice.

By that night's performance in the Student Commons in Binghamton, Cage had already been creating for four decades and had established himself as a major force in the discourse around musical composition specifically and art making in general.

Indeterminacy, the work I respond to in *Story/Time*, had its first presentation in Brussels in 1958. I fixate on Cage as opposed to, say, Marcel Duchamp, who arguably made Cage's contribution possible, because Cage in his homespun, American way identified strongly with time-based art, music, and dance. Why not focus instead on Merce Cunningham, one of the choreographers

I have learned most from—a great master whose assimilation of Cage's ideas changed the landscape I was to walk into? Perhaps Merce is too close. His form, though much different from mine, is at once too familiar and too particular for my purposes in this book. The discourse I am engaging with is better personified by the singular figure of John Cage, a theoretician, lightning rod, and giver of permissions. I choose Cage because as an icon he is better able to absorb all the symbolism and significations I direct at this tradition I have labored so long to be a part of.

Let's say John Cage is water and Merce, one of the wonderful beverages one might make of it.

Culture is sometimes defined as "the well-stocked mind." By that definition, on that night in the Student Commons I suffered a severe cultural deficit! I came from what today would be called the working poor: agricultural workers from a farming community in the Finger Lakes region of New York State that—like so much of the country—benefited from the prosperity and optimism of the '50s and '60s. The culture we absorbed in my family, recently transplanted from the South, was standard American fare: TV, radio, magazines all inflected by African American folklore, religion, and social rituals such as play-acting, dancing and singing, and entertaining ourselves with the new stereo player and the jukebox that at one point resided in our living room. The public school I had graduated from had the typical mandatory curriculum in the arts: literature, required reading of Emily Dickinson, Robert Frost, Melville's *Moby Dick*, Mark Twain's *Huckleberry Finn*. It offered several varieties of sports,

a good choral program, a high school band and—essential for me—a drama club: the opportunity to perform plays or musicals that might have recently been seen or revived on Broadway.

Much has changed in my thinking since I decided to attempt *Story/Time*. Now, having made the work, premiered it, and toured it, I have only begun to appreciate the misapprehensions brought on by art historical traditions and my own place within them.

When I began work on *Story/Time*, I considered John Cage to be *the* icon of modernism—when in fact this is a label that should be shared with other mid-twentieth-century New York composers and theoreticians such as Morton Feldman, Christian Wolf, and Earl Brown. Historian/critic/writer John Rockwell, in a searching dialog we had recently, was adamant in correcting this misapprehension, reminding me that as far as reigning schools of musical modernism were concerned, there were at least three:

- The Darmstadt, Germany, post-Webern and post-Schoenberg school of atonality.
- The US version of this twelve-tone group as represented by Milton Babbitt.
- A branch of the New York School as represented by Cage, Feldman, Wolf, et al., who were caught in a pitched battle for the mantle of "truly advanced" music composition with what Morton Feldman titled the "academic avant-garde" that Babbitt represented.

So I concede to John Rockwell that John Cage was but one voice. But to my thinking he was the most singular. Certainly not because of the popularity of his compositions—judged by who is most played on the concert stages of the world today, Morton Feldman remains far more popular. But Cage remains more consequential because of the influence his thoughts had and continue to have on generations of artists in many disciplines.

> We are not, in these dances and music, saying something. We are simple minded enough to think that if we were saying something we would use words. We are rather doing something. . . .
>
> The movement is the movement of the body. . . . Here, however, we are in the presence of a dance, which utilizes the entire body, requiring for its enjoyment the use of your faculty of kinesthetic sympathy. It is this faculty we employ when, seeing the flight of birds, we ourselves, by identification, fly up, glide, and soar.
>
> The novelty of our work derives therefore from our having moved away from simply private human concerns towards the world of nature and society of which all of us are a part. Our intention is to affirm this life, not to bring order out of chaos nor to suggest improvements in creation, but simply to wake up to the very life we are living, which is so

excellent once one gets one's mind and one's desires out of its way and lets it act of its own accord.

John Cage speaking of the Cunningham Company, *In This Day*, from *Silence*

I concede that I have been making Cage into a sort of straw man, a stand-in for a school of thought and a culture that I did not understand well and felt excluded from . . .

I mentioned earlier that Cage's *Indeterminacy* is both a comfort and a provocation to me. Let's take a moment to look at an important and controversial aspect of Cage's view of this work. First, he saw the act of composition, the execution of the composition, and the experience of the auditors as separate activities. It is said that Cage assigns a higher priority to the author's intent or choices of presentation than to the audience's capacity to interpret that intent.

And here the provocation:

Sri Ramakrishna was once asked, "Why, if God is good, is there evil in the world?" He said, "In order to thicken the plot."

Paraphrasing the question put to Sri Ramakrishna and the answer he gave, I would ask this: "Why, if anything is possible, do we concern ourselves with history (in other words with the sense of what is necessary to be done at a particular time)?" And I

would answer, "In order to thicken the plot." In this view, then, all those interpenetrations, which seem at first glance to be hellish—history, for instance, if we are speaking of experimental music—are to be espoused. One does not then make just any experiment but does what must be done. By this I mean one does not seek by his actions to arrive at money, but does what must be done; one does not seek by his action to arrive at fame (success) but does what must be done; one does not seek by his actions to provide pleasure to the senses (beauty) but does what must be done; one does not seek by his actions to arrive at the establishment of a school (truth) but does what must be done. One does something else. What else?

John Cage, *History of Experimental Music in the United States*

For an artist like myself, at times described as an "artiste engagé"; i.e., a socially engaged artist—with an emotional and expressionistic bent who places a high premium on spontaneity and improvisation while striving for success, Cage's claiming of the mantle of what is truly advanced, i.e., most necessary—is a provocation.

Leaving a show of Pat Steir's work called Winter Paintings *at Cheim & Read Gallery, I thought back some years to when the Walker Art Center's then curator Richard Flood was walking us through the Center's collection and we came upon an abstract expressionist painting by Joan Mitchell that was so striking I asked him why it had taken so long for her to be recognized. He answered with a wry expression: "It's the problem of beauty!"*

A few days earlier our friends Kol and Dash came to lunch at our home, and Dash said that at this time most visual art is conceptual. "It's a way of thinking," she said.

But it is also a comfort. The comfort is in giving oneself permission: to please oneself first, to not be understood—even to not be liked.

In the spring of 2011 I saw *Sleep No More*, a performance by the London-based Punch Drunk Theater Company. It is an inspired theater performance/interactive event wherein a small army of actors, dancers, designers, and various facilitators provide a rambling, open-ended experience. A man (or was it a woman?) informed us before we were let in that "you will be directed, but not told what you will experience"—a sentiment Cage would have applauded. We were led into an astonishingly complex warren of rooms and spaces of various dimensions and an incomprehensible number of carefully crafted installations. Much of the time it was dark, with a wondrous and everpresent sound design of ambient noise, ballads, and popular music from the first half of the twentieth century. All spectators were required to wear masks and were instructed not to talk under any circumstance, creating an odd sense of anonymity and vulnerability that became more comfortable and illuminating as time wore on.

As the event unfolded, one encountered various scenes between a number of attractive ensemble players. Often a performer would dash away to another location. This sudden movement pulled in its wake a school of masked spectators, sometimes literally running to keep up with the elusive player. Several times I tailed the group, and when I encountered a fork in the road providing me the option of either following the crowd or venturing another course, I often chose to follow the crowd.

At times one was close enough to literally touch a performer or to see a performer thinking. It's at such moments one rediscovers a larger truth about theater, one that was challenged by certain modernist/postmodern choreographers and is still being examined today, and that is: What is artifice? What is the value of pretending? In *Sleep No More* there came a moment when I stood in a group of maybe twenty masked spectators watching a woman at a small table eating. Because most of us were made invisible by our masked anonymity, this woman, this actor, was the only human among us revealed, and yet she was in character, shrouded in artifice and behaving as the only "real" human being, though she was herself pretending. So this is what theater is!

These reminiscences take me back to a recognition of the creed I inherited from John Cage. Just as he is supposed to have encouraged Merce Cunningham to leave Martha Graham because "that woman is becoming too literary"—that is, too much about acting/drama and not enough about the elemental truth of the act of dancing—so Cage is known to have said he was not interested in symbolism because he preferred things to "be just what they are." The question is, what are things?

During a snowstorm, Cecil Taylor, Arnie Zane, and I stepped into the Blue Note, shaking off the snow in the uncanny stillness of Sixth Avenue.

Cecil introduced us to an array of personalities, some well known, all lovers of jazz, and Abbey Lincoln in particular, who sat quietly at the bar between sets. This was the treat Cecil had promised us earlier that evening. We had met at the insistence of Max Roach, who envisaged a collaboration between Cecil, himself, and the two of us for the Brooklyn Academy of Music's brand-new Next Wave Festival.

Meeting with Cecil he had quickly dismissed Max as "that old bebop drummer" and passionately insisted we consider Abbey Lincoln instead, as he was more than intrigued by her style and "this thing she does, past words, past singing."

He kept repeating, "Man, it's a sound she makes. A sound . . ."

John Cage is certainly my "straw man." My self, my creative self, struggles to connect to a way of thinking, a modernist tradition, and—more precisely—the New York School John Cage became a leader of.

Cage's body of work and, most importantly, the philosophy and practice that inform it elicit a set of responses in me, a maker, who continues in Cage's wake. Yes, I am listening to the work, but I am also encountering the individual. This individual's specificity elicits a response as well, sometimes personal.

December in the Casita.

I decided that each afternoon I would do a minimum of two tasks: work on an upcoming address and listen to one of an eight-CD boxed set of John Cage reading Diary: How to Improve the World (You Will Only Make Matters Worse).

I resigned myself to allow the torrent of Cage's ideas, quotations, anecdotes, and isolated words to rush over my mind and ears.

One day a word made me stop the CD player, go back, and transcribe what I had just heard.

The story was:

Pia Gilbert, born in Southern Germany, got into a taxi cab in NYC. The driver said, "I am a Black Muslim."

She replied, "I am sorry to hear it."

—"You don't believe in the truth?"

—"That isn't the truth."

—"You don't like negroes?"

—"What makes you think I am not a negro?"

What are things, really? What is the self, really?

Everyone today who sets out to prove an ultimate truth or provide the unassailable argument for a point of view will be challenged and, ultimately, humbled if not humiliated. We all remember a recent electoral season in which one side accused the other of existing in a "reality-based culture" now declared passé by its "new/old" revelation of "will to change reality" or the "inspiration of faith." We're all witness to the debate around global warming with a majority of eminent scientists and researchers saying it is real while a small, potent group exerts a dismaying drag on the question by exploiting the media and encouraging many to denounce facts in favor of feeling . . . the need to "feel" they will never need to change.

In the face of our era's tsunami of relativism, I maintain that there is value in the idea of a true and authentic self. Why? Perhaps it is my Southern Baptist infrastructure inherited from the exhortations of my mother and father, self-anointed "Black Yankees" who traveled North in search of "big money"—handpicking 100 pounds of potatoes at 12 cents a bag—as opposed to cutting cabbage in the South for less. Perhaps it is this economic optimism marinated in the euphoric rhetoric of the Civil Rights Movement, saying "We shall overcome." One of the earliest memories I have is literally standing between my Dad's knees probably tracing or sounding out on a roadmap "Little Rock" well before I could actually read. Or joining all the folk around the new TV set as firehoses and dogs assaulted people that looked like us and hearing those staring at the screen saying under their breath, "Lawd! Lawd! You all go on now! Go on!" to the tiny soaked and terrorized black and white figures in this most harrowing dance performance. Perhaps it was the queasy-making slant on righteousness that encouraged my parents to

congratulate an older brother, little more than a child, who had produced a shotgun to chase away the man from the electric company come to turn off the electricity and gas for lack of payment one dreary late winter evening when they were still away at work. "We ain't no thieves," said my father, "it just ain't right to cut off our gas with a house full of children and it's cold outside."

Perhaps all of the above is why it was such a heart-stopping relief to hear the music of the 60s declaring, "We got a revolution! We want a revolution!" accompanied by images of giddy young people blithely dancing, protesting, claiming that the old order was dead and that "they"—soon to be "we," as I would join them—were (like the times) a-changing. Perhaps it was this that said it was OK to leave the sexual trajectory that had carried my family forever and take a white woman and then a white man into my arms in the conviction that I had every right to hold hands with her or him in public, and every intention to defend that right with violence if challenged.

Perhaps all of the above willed me in my art to make larger, inclusive statements such as: "If we stand together naked on the stage, we will have overcome," whatever divides us. "If we use a dance concert as an opportunity for a disparate group of individuals to create something and show it to the largest audience possible, we will have triumphed over the fear and doubt that divide us."

If I am brave enough to reveal the most personal aspects of myself, I reasoned, others will do the same. What will result is something akin to the supplicant calling out in distress or joy to the congregation, and the congregation, the community, returning a full-throated affirmation, "We hear you! We are not afraid! We shall overcome!"

But I don't feel this so unequivocally at this time . . . I may feel it again, but not so strongly right now. I will go so far as to say that all my efforts, my ideas, and my feelings are in question.

Years ago Senta Driver, a brilliant woman and a former dancer in Paul Taylor's troupe, told me that John Cage had undergone a crisis in the 1940s, a sort of breakdown that prevented him from making decisions. He turned to Zen Buddhism and chance procedures instead. We now know that Cage's crisis was complex and real.

It was both a personal crisis and a professional crisis. . . . I would not say it was a crisis because he couldn't make choices, but because he found himself in a situation where what he was doing wasn't working. That showed up in a couple of ways. One was his shift of emotions from Xenia, his wife, to Merce Cunningham, so it was the breakdown of a marriage out of which he composed "The Perilous Night," which is about "when love goes wrong." I think that's his quote, or "when romance becomes unhappy" or something like that. So it was the breakdown of his marriage, it was the war and the onset of the Cold War period, and his questioning what was the value of being a composer in that kind of a world where there was unemployment and there was so much social strife and there was so much war. What good was it to be a composer to try and convey emotions? He thought there were quite enough emotions in the world all by themselves. It didn't need him.

I don't know that it was a crisis of not being able to make choices, but realizing that the choices made may or may not be the right choices. So the choices themselves or the idea of choices were somewhat arbitrary. He wanted to find something underneath that.

Laura Kuhn, Director, John Cage Trust

Was I—am I—in crisis as I turn to indeterminacy and chance procedure in *Story/Time*? Difficult to say. On one hand, things are better than ever for me, professionally and personally. I regularly receive support and recognition for my work. Bill T. Jones/ Arnie Zane Dance Company continues to exist and thrive. We have merged with the historic Dance Theater Workshop (DTW) to form a new entity called New York Live Arts as a means of finding a permanent home and to revisit the mission of a venerable research center and safe haven for the untried and unexposed in contemporary live arts, embodied research, and contemporary

dance performance. I have extended my creativity into the area of commercial theater and have been welcomed there. On the other hand, success has sometimes brought with it crippling doubt in the face of stiff winds of criticism, some of which is malicious and calculated to undercut and destroy. My dancer's body is retired, but the dancer's ego is often bereft.

My self is a sort of field where my work originates or certainly must struggle to be made. It can be described by the various voices that originate there. Most—if not all—the voices are me talking to myself. Others are personalities like thinkers, fellow creators, and critics who may or may not be actual persons. Sometimes they are aggregates, fictional/created entities that appear to me to be speaking to each other as if I were not there, or more painfully as if I were a comatose patient in a hospital room over whom my caregivers and family are commiserating. The din is frightening. So, yes, indeterminacy, *Story/Time*, are refuge from all of the above.

Max Roach told of the day when Abbey Lincoln and he were excitedly putting the finishing touches on a Thelonius Monk tune to which Abbey had written lyrics. They were excited because Monk himself was to come by. He came, listened intently to their performance, whispered something into Abbey's ear, and then left.

Max asked her what Monk had said. And here Max, doing a perfect imitation of Monk's curiously gruff, gravelly speech, whispered, "Next time, make a mistake!"

Human existence is—or at least might be—less troubling and more peaceful if individuals went about their daily lives without expectations, only experiences and awareness.

Rama Krishna

I find it hard to agree with Rama Krishna's advice encouraging us to go about our daily lives without expectations, for it clashes with lived experience such as my parents' teachings that one must earn a living, stay out of jail, and be responsible for one's choices in all things.

How did *Story/Time* come about? A few years ago, having produced with my Associate Director, Janet Wong, my dancers, and a loyal group of collaborators on average one or two evening-length works a year over a ten-year period, and having participated in the creation of one off-Broadway and two successful Broadway shows and about to gear up for a third, I decided that I wanted to perform again myself. (I had retired from dancing some five years earlier.) My plan was to make something with and for my company of nine dancers and something for myself. For myself it was to be "small-scale," low-key, and crafted for art spaces or small theaters. It would not involve dancing, as I had had knee surgery and back problems. It would be an opportunity to do what I love: sing and tell stories. More than fatigued with the ongoing need to sell tickets and to stay vital in the dance-touring world, this project would not have the same commercial

expectations. It would not aspire to be performed in the venues the company normally appears in.

The work for myself became the work for the company, causing much to change in scale, resources, and presentation. Why? I suppose because that project held the most fascination for me, a condition that always drives the need to make something new. Until that moment at least . . .

I had for some years been listening to Cage's 1978 recording of *Indeterminacy* to relax. His voice and the rambling, often peculiar subject matter were a delightful respite. It suddenly struck me that I was full of stories of my own and didn't want to organize them with a preconceived structure or arc. I decided that for this work I would read about 70 one-minute-long stories (randomly selected from a pool of over 170) while my dancers performed around me.

Here was an opportunity to be direct and sincere while still able to "float," as Roland Barthes is known to have said in the face of relentless requests for his position on almost everything. While inspired by *Indeterminacy*, *Story/Time* would be a system of my making in which I could participate at a remove, like the spectator, but differently in that I would never witness the result as the spectator does.

The company would be given a broad menu of movement sequences ranging from those borrowed from works created almost thirty years ago to those created on the day of each performance. Because sequences were subjected to minute-long durations (some running longer than that), they can be and are joined differently as their order is selected using www.random.org as opposed to John Cage's tossing of coins and consulting the *I Ching*.

Get rid of the glue!

Henry Cowell

In *Story/Time*, transitions are nonexistent or abrupt, meaning each performer, myself included, must stay focused, alert, and infinitely adaptable. Through chance procedure the structure remains ever fresh and challenging for the dancers, for our lighting and stage crew, for composer Ted Coffey, for me, and for the audience.

Terrifying and exciting!

Indeterminacy and *Story/Time* are a respite from my usual way of working. I had come through several very difficult years of research and construction of a large public spectacle called *Fondly Do We Hope, Fervently Do We Pray* and I was tired. I was also full of doubt. And I must admit that my struggles to craft a work like *Fondly. . . .* left me desiring a means to create past my limitations of memory and taste. Cage's work in general, and *Indeterminacy* in particular, offered a welcome new way forward.

Why keep connecting him with his work? Don't you see that he's a human being whereas his work isn't? If for instance you decided to kick his work and him, you would wouldn't you have to perform two actions rather than a single one. The more he leaves his work the more useable it becomes. . . . Room in it for others."

John Cage, *Diary: How to Improve the World (You Will Only Make Matters Worse)*

I have found a comfort and a provocation as well in the philosophy that led John Cage to *Indeterminacy*, and I respect that he never insisted that performers become disciples—"little Cagettes," as John Rockwell puts it—in their creation.

I have found Cage, the man and the artist/theoretician, to be a harsh mentor, giving permission on one hand, but stern and disapproving as well:

The strength that comes from firmly established art practices is not present in the modern dance today. Insecure, not having any clear direction, the modern dancer is willing to compromise and to accept influences from other more rooted art manners, enabling one to remark that certain dancers are either borrowing from or selling themselves to Broadway, others are learning from folk or Oriental arts, and many are introducing into their work elements of the ballet or, in an all-out effort, devoting themselves to it. Confronted with its history, its former power, its present insecurity, the

realization is unavoidable that the strength the modern dance once had was not impersonal but was intimately connected with and ultimately depended on the personality and even the actual physical bodies of the individuals who imparted it.

John Cage, *Grace and Clarity* (1944), from *Silence*

When Cage reads his wonderful one-minute stories, they are plotted out by the second. As *Story/Time* is very much a work in progress, Ted Coffey, my musical collaborator, has set some of my stories in such a time frame, but—for the most part—I intuit my reading of each story, I improvise my way through each minute.

Chance operations are a discipline, and improvisation is rarely a discipline. Though at the present time it's one of my concerns, how to make improvisation a discipline. But then I mean doing something beyond the control of the ego. Improvisation is generally playing what you know, and what you like, and what you feel; but those feelings and likes are what Zen would like us to become free of.

John Cage, in conversation with Stanley Kauffmann (1966)

The wonder of Cage is that he can be so categorical and yet always exploratory and open. Twenty years after the preceding quote he said:

If you have work to do that is suggested but not determined by a notation, if it's indeterminate, this simply means that you are to supply the determination of certain things that the composer has not determined.

Cage thus opens the door to improvisation.

But does he open the door to intention as opposed to non-intention? One of the most troubling but fruitful realities of *Story/Time* was that unlike Cage's own production *Indeterminacy*, my stories were not consistently arranged by random procedure. Some stories and sequences were so important to me that they were given a certain pride of place nightly, complete with crafted lighting and even sound. Why? Because there was a "feeling" I had that I insisted on preserving and sharing with an audience. Having made this decision with the help of my Associate Director, Janet Wong, we were free to make the work that we felt it "necessary" to make. And here I turn to my mentor, who has said that the first importance to the composer is to find something new. I counter by saying that is certainly important, but just as important is that the composer finds something—rather than original—authentic.

I dreamed of the old house I grew up in on Miller Road. It was almost dark and it might have been a Saturday night because the house was empty, peaceful. I was alone in the kitchen with my father, much older than he would have been at that time. We sat quietly, me holding his hand, massaging it.

I asked if that helped him.

His eyes were sad and smiling.

He said gently, "That feels real good!"

* * *

My mother, Estella, died in the fall of 2002. Though she was to be buried near her mother, Anna, in the small town of Bunnell, Florida, the funeral service was held in Tampa.

The service was the culmination of a week of grieving outbursts, negotiations, hurt feelings, and, certainly, laughter. However, when the minister, after a moving though perfunctory eulogy, said to us, Estella's children, "You all come to say goodbye to your Mama," everything changed.

Ten out of twelve of us were present, standing around the open coffin. I was sure this would be a purely public formality even as I heard the low murmur of my siblings addressing our mother, each in a private voice. These quiet calls took on urgency close to hysteria as the coffin's lid was slowly closing. Some even tried to stop it.

I felt secure in the role of observer until the wailing was joined by one more voice crying, pleading for more time to look, to touch.

It was my voice . . .

Story/Time is an evening-length work made for my ten-member company on a spare stage designed by Bjorn Amelan with a sound-score created by composer Ted Coffey and sound design by Sam Crawford. Initially this work, a response to John Cage's 1958 *Indeterminacy*, was to have been for myself—a lone reader in the middle of an empty space, reading an hour-plus of one-minute stories I have written in front of a small audience, with the participation of Ted Coffey. For various reasons, the company work eclipsed this initial idea.

When the schedule at Princeton made Richardson Auditorium unavailable for the second of my three performance-lectures, we were obliged to move to a smaller space, a lecture hall with a very small stage and a blackboard. I decided to make this limitation a virtue and fashioned an event complete with lighting design and soundscape that would heighten the experience of this sixty minutes and make it somehow more singular and resonant. Having sat over many years watching Bjorn Amelan in the private exercise of drawing, I thought it would be an interesting, indeterminate conversation if he would draw on the blackboard behind me.

The stories that follow are numbered according to the order in which they have been written. They were chosen by chance procedure using www.random.org and set in 60-second grids by Ted Coffey following John Cage's example.

2A

0″ At Copenhagen's Opera House there came a moment in tech rehearsal when the majority of dancers were to stand still in a close group watching one woman performing a solo.   A dancer at the front of the clump quietly began to draw

10″ attention to something of concern on the floor. The group's focus changed and everyone joined in, gesturing and commenting in an ever-rising murmur.   Someone was bleeding.

20″ Observing them examining themselves and each other was like watching a pack catching the scent of prey. The soloist continued her movements as one man broke from the group and

30″ dashed into the wings. Returning a moment later, clutching paper towels, he went to work on the spots of blood. I could see that at any moment the others might break rank as well.   I asked him to rejoin the formation, as the group was soon to resume

40″ dancing.   Fortunately several crewmembers had gotten the message and were down on hands and knees working at the blood.   Around them, refocused and alert, the dance continued.

50″ The scene was bathed in a beautiful light.   It was strange and lovely.

0″

John Cowles was in the final stage of lung cancer.

We went to visit him and Sage in their lovely loft in Minneapolis. John greeted us in his bathrobe.

10″

He was unshaven. There was an extremely long plastic tube connecting him to an oxygen tank. Still,

over the twenty years I have known him, he had never been more dashing and full of fun. He insisted we

20″

drink champagne with him, popping the cork on a second bottle before we left.

30″

In the hallway, near the elevator, was a poster of *Last Supper at Uncle Tom's Cabin*

40″

/ *The Promised Land.*

It has faded over the years. We remarked to John that perhaps he might want to preserve it as it

50″

has become something of a collector's item. With a mischievous smile and a shrug, he said simply: "Après moi…"

22

0"

10"

It was sundown in the summer of 1972 and Arnie Zane and I were standing,

hitchhiking on the NY State Thruway trying to get a ride home to Brockport from Buffalo. The

State Troopers had already threatened

20"

arrest if they caught us standing where we were. We had retreated up

the ramp, but decided to risk going back as night was falling.

30"

For the week prior, we had been at

New Brindavan, the Krishna Consciousness retreat in West Virginia, chanting and praying from before dawn

40"

to late into the night. The rhythmic clanging of cymbals, pounding of drums and ecstatic shouts of "Govinda

Jiah! Jiah! Gopahla Jiah! Jiah!" — "Govinda Jiah! Jiah! Gopahla Jiah! Jiah!" were still ringing in my ears, mixed

50"

with the whoosh and roar of sixteen-wheelers, family cars, and buses.

We were very small, very high, and very alert as the stars came out.

0″

10″ Yesterday at Chicago's Art Institute looking at a pile of

candies —

20″ a work by Félix Gonzáles-Torres — the audio-guide explained that

the pile of brightly colored sweets represented for the artist the body of his deceased friend.

30″ Visitors were invited to take one, to participate in the feasting that would devour us all.

Today, just past dawn, leaving Chicago I crawl into the backseat of

40″ a black sedan hired to take me to the airport. In the armrest

between the seats are two unopened bottles of water, two packets of "oil-controlling

50″ towelets,"

and two brightly wrapped hard candies.

0″ I dreamed of the old house I grew up in on Miller Road.

10″

20″

30″ It was almost dark and it might have been a Saturday night because the house was empty, peaceful. I was

40″ alone in the kitchen with my father, much older than he would have been at that time. We sat quietly, me holding his hand, massaging

50″ it. I asked him if that helped him. His eyes were sad and smiling. He said gently, "That feels real good!"

65

0″ In the summer of 1993,

Arthur, Bjorn, and I were visiting Walter de Maria's Lightening Fields in southern NM.

10″ We had reserved all six places in the guesthouse so we would have privacy.

In the morning, Arthur had gone walking among the lightening rods;

20″ I was

daydreaming when Bjorn called me to his room to help him with a panicked vivid green hummingbird

30″ fluttering against the mosquito screen. A short while later, he had gently captured

it and was cupping it in his hand when he offered it to me to do the same before we

40″ released it out the front door.

I have seldom held a thing so fragile, so dependent on my care.

50″ I would like to think — as it grew quiet and still — it trusted me,

though even now I can recall the rapid beating of its heart on my palm.

26

0″ At some point in the late '80s, Betty Freeman rented Alice Tully Hall for one night so as to present the music of Lou Harrison, which had not been heard in NY for some time.

10″ It was a major event in the music world and in the crowd was Virgil Thomson who had known Lou Harrison for many years.

20″

Lou Harrison took the stage in a bubbly, flamboyant manner, describing in lengthy detail his pre-

30″ occupation with the music of Asia as opposed to the tyranny of "that small tip of Asia Minor we call Europe."

40″

Virgil, seated alone swathed in an extravagant colorful Afghani robe,

50″ which Bill Katz had just wrapped him in, shouted out at the top of his voice:

"Talk, talk, talk . . . When do we hear the music?"

28

0"
{ The mountains cup the mesas as I look northeast toward Taos,

10"
{ caught in the harsh last rays on this first day of 2012.
Taos, the sacred Blue Mountain, the pylons, the spindly power lines,

20"
{ and the grey-green sagebrush are stripped naked and apparent.
I can see the bare outline of Highway 68 in the distance and, even more improbably,

30"
{ individual cars and trucks, insect-like as the sunset catches on glass, metal, and chrome.
I am here on the mesa because I do not want to be in that small city,

40"
{ or any city, today. Yet I grow obsessed with identifying man-made
landmarks 10, 20, 30 miles away or following those metal

50"
{ insects that seem to alight, take off, or hover around, and through the
distant drift of landscape evermore abandoned by the retreating sunlight.

0" { It was the end of a festive lunch, full of stories, wine, and good food.

I was talking with my friend Peter and he was saying how

10" { moved he had been to see a short documentary about

my work on television.

20" {

30" { He loved seeing the

dancing, but the footage of Arnie and me performing *A*

40" { *Study for Valley Cottage* some thirty- plus years ago disturbed him.

When I asked him why, he said uncomfortably, "I wish I had been there.

50" { I wish I had seen you guys then. Why did it have to look so old..."

0" It was Saturday morning in 1972.   I had left Arnie relaxing in a patch of sunlight on the front stoop of our

tenement   dressed in pink pedal pushers and a polka-dotted peasant-blouse.   His thick dark hair was free

10" and luxurious.   I returned a few hours later. His outfit, like his demeanor, had become darkly masculine.

His hair was pulled severely back.   "What happened?" I asked.   It seems that a car full of young

20" teenage men had started harassing him.   Arnie had picked up a large, heavy metal drawer   from a pile of

junk   and hurled it across a lane of highway,   damaging   their car.   The driver screamed   that he was

30" going to get the police. Arnie dashed upstairs   to adjust his   appearance.   Before long   the damaged car

appeared,   followed by a police vehicle.   As the young driver   opened   his mouth, Arnie   announced,

40" "Officer,   I would like to file charges   against   these young men."   The young driver's   eyes   bulged.

As he stammered,   the policeman   ordered   him to shut up, get back in the car,

50" and show his license.   The cop turned   to Arnie, saying,   "I am so sorry, sir.

It's a shame with these young people.   The parents are the problem."

154

On the mesa, a group of us stood together,   looking into the   distance,   watching

10" the sunset more   intently than   usual   because Richard   had   said:

"If   you   look   closely   enough,   just   at   the   moment   when   the   sun   goes

20" below   the   horizon,   the   sky   makes   a   peculiar   change   and   turns   neon   green."

30"

40"

I   joined   them   in   this,   but   became   so   involved   in   looking   at

50" my   friends   looking   that   by   the   time   I   turned   back   to   the   sun,   it   was   down   and   all   I

caught   was   its   familiar   glow   behind   the   black   line   of   the   mountains.

31

0" { In 1999 we premiered a work in three parts called *We Set Out Early…*

Visability Was Poor. The second section, *Cape Bardo,* was performed

10" { to a recording of John Cage performing *Empty Words* at the Teatro Lirico in Milan.

The audience of revolutionary students began to riot in

20" { response to Cage's reading *Walden Pond* — not the text as written, but phonemes or

word fragments chosen by chance procedure.

30" {

Later, over dinner, Stephen Wright — a manager

40" { of symphony orchestras — said of both Cage and Schoenberg:

"For practically seventy years conductors and impresarios have been trying

50" { to force this stuff on audiences. When will they realize people just don't like it?

Audiences simply don't want it. It doesn't work!"

0″
It was March. A
light snow was falling. "Usuyuki" the Japanese call it.

10″
And though I was grateful for the heartbreaking

20″
beauty on
weighted bamboo, the latticework of budding trees, and the frosted

30″
granite boulders — I fell into
comparing this March evening to another one 24 years ago when

40″
it was warmer, forsythias were in bloom everywhere
as the neighborhood seemed to be holding its breath,

50″
and Arnie was dying upstairs in the bedroom.
That would always be March.

0" { I had not spoken to Lillie Mae since her husband, Harris, my eldest brother, died a few

few years before. I was calling to locate family photos of the 1940s, '50s, and '60s

10" { for various documentary projects. Lillie Mae was very warm. She told me he had

hidden the photographs as his Alzeimer progressed, and — though she had looked for them

20" { after his death — she had no idea where they could be. She spoke of her initial skepticism at

the idea that there was anything wrong with his mind. That changed the day he walked out of the house,

30" { waving his children away dismissively as they called to him, asking where he was going. He grew ever

more fearful, often hiding outside in the bushes. He became violent, striking her in the face once

40" { as she asked him to sit down for lunch. She was obliged to hide all knives and an old shotgun

he would sit out front holding. When the end came, though he barely recognized her, he tried

50" { to hold her hand, only able to grasp two fingers. She quietly encouraged him to let go. She

knew he had passed when he released her hand and was still.

0" At the opening of a new concert hall in Dortmund, Germany, dignitaries were in attendance. It was to be an all Beethoven program.

10" At one point the music stopped as Professor Wapnewski, an elderly man with spectacles and white tousled hair, proceeded to

20" speak in German. Members of the orchestra and chorus sat perfectly still until they, like everyone in the room, realized that he was going to speak

30" for a very long time and they began to fidget. At least two people, way up high in the chorus, fell asleep. Later, Bjorn, who speaks the language, tried to

40" reconstruct highlights of the speech. It seems it had been about honor, language, culture, tolerance. There was one thing that sticks with me, although

50" I am not sure I got it right. "We believe society should offer freedom and equality, yet freedom is the permission to be individual and individuality is the opposite of equality."

36

0"

As a plane

flies over a city,

10"

there comes a moment when one looks out

20"

and tries to recognize distinct objects

below: a train

30"

or a semi-truck — smaller than a matchbox . . . then later, a person maybe.

40"

We don't have a reason for this. Sometimes the one on the ground looks up.

They probably hear the engines first,

50"

or see our shadow.

136

0"　In *Diary:　How to Improve the World　(You Will Only Make Matters Worse)*　Cage says:

"They taught us art was self-expression　—　you had to have something　to say.　They were wrong.

10"

You don't have to say anything.

20"

Think of the others as artists...

Art is self-alteration."

30"

I have stopped　the Cage CD number

4　several　times　today,

most often

40"　to go back and write down something　he said.

Just now　I stopped　it

to　write　what　I am thinking　and that is a question:

50"　Out of all the many　things　he reports,　do I get involved　only　with　those

I agree　with　or with those　that make me　uneasy?

0" On a warm late spring day of 1992 in Prague I took a crowded bus with my mother, Estella, and Arthur Aviles to the Theresienstadt concentration camp. Unfortunately, the bus did not go to the camp itself,

10" but instead dropped the three of us in the village nearby and left us to beg a ride as best we could.

Stunned, we sat on a bench in the deserted square. Eventually a couple of German tourists gave us

20" a ride to the camp memorial. It seemed deserted. I remember little about the immense place, other than the green of its gently rolling hills and the many stone markers scattered across the landscape.

30" Estella didn't understand the significance of the place and assumed I had made this difficult journey to take her to a cemetary. We

40" strolled around for a while, and then sat on a bench under a tree to rest. Estella, fanning her broad, sweating face with a handkerchief declared: "Son, I've always heard that if you really

50" wanted to learn to pick the guitar, you got to work at it all night in a graveyard. Oh, yes! Sure enough the next day you'll be able to pick John Henry. You'll be able to play that thing!"

38

61

0" { I was watching an amateur pornographic film and it was striking because of the assignment of roles. All the participants were African American. It seemed that a

10" { group of women had hired a man to entertain them. The women were in their late thirties or forties and ample of body, well coiffed, and having a great time. The man was handsome

20" { with a generous endowment and he behaved as if in an erotic trance, going from one fully clothed woman to the next, lying down on them, rubbing his body in a childlike way on

30" { their breasts, on their stomachs. At one moment, his naked bottom was in the face of one of the laughing women who playfully patted

40" { it, complimenting him on the shape of his buttocks as she would a small child.

50" { Later another woman fondled his penis, laughing for her own and her friends' enjoyment, saying, "That's so nice, just look at it!"

0″ { Betty Freeman was a great friend to contemporary music and a friend

of mine. I met her at Bill Katz's loft the same night I met John Cage. She

10″ { sat next to Cage at the far end of a long table, between him and Jasper Johns. As

Arnie and I entered the room, she asked Bill, "Who is that? He's a dancer,

20″ { right?" Bill sat me near her and John. At one point she asked Cage to

tell a story. As he began speaking she interrupted saying, "Not that one, John.

30″ { The other one." Now, after thirty years, I can't remember either story…

40″ {

50″ {

40

0" Flooded McDonalds:

A brightly lit McDonalds being slowly flooded gave a wicked, vindictive pleasure as

10" french-fries fell in the water, then floated to the surface. It was hilarious

witnessing a "Happy Meal" carton amid soaked hamburger buns caught in a

20" small whirlpool cascading past the Coke machine.

One catches one's breath,

30" and then laughs out loud

as the cash machine explodes in the rising muck. The red, yellow, and white room

40" fills

50" till all the lights blow out and the camera takes us underwater where the dead food

and garbage become somber, sad, and mysterious.

0″

10″

20″

I was rehearsing my solo show at Aaron Davis Hall's Studio B

one Saturday morning. Estella was visiting us from San Francisco and sat quietly

30″ in a row of chairs,

watching me dancing to a

40″ recording of Dietrich Fischer-Diskau singing Schubert's *Litanei auf das Fest Aller Seelen* (*Litany*

for All Soul's Day). Knowing she was no fan of German Romantic music and suspecting

50″ she was only slightly more interested in what I would do to it, I assumed Estella was not

watching. However, when I stopped, she said: "That one I like. It was so pretty!"

0″ Every year, from approximately the middle of December to the first week of January, Bjorn and I spend time on the mesa of northern

10″ New Mexico. It's quiet and open there with mountains all around. The sky shifts constantly, as does the wind and the light. Still, one

20″ has the impression that nothing changes. In fact it feels like the sort of place one might create in the future when we can

30″ custom-make a virtual vacation spot. One afternoon, halfway through my holiday, I was determined to listen to John Cage read *Indeterminacy* *Part II* for

40″ inspiration and as a means of getting away from the list of things, people, and feelings inside of me. In the mesa light and

50″ quiet I was writing this story as I was listening to his recording, attempting to name the very things I was trying to forget.

0″

I saw a show of Pat Steir's paintings at Cheim & Read Gallery. They were large format paintings, juxtaposing two vertical panels of color.

20″

Sometimes one of the color panels was hidden behind a curtain of streaming paint of another color. At other times, the streaming curtain covered both halves.

30″

But it was at the center seam where the two panels met that the cascading rivulets and streaks were most dramatic — like tears, perhaps.

40″

They were called *Winter Paintings*.

50″

As we stepped into the street, it was raining, cold and overcast. It was the third day of spring.

0″   At Bard College   during a lull in rehearsal   in Theatre

10″   2, I was leaving the stage as dancer   LaMichael was returning   to it, applying   a Band-Aid to his

finger.   "Battle wound?" I asked,   assuming   he had done it just now in rehearsal.

20″   "No, I did it at breakfast — " walking   away from him I turned   as he continued   " — but it was an

accident."

30″   I think it was a joke.

    Still   I had a momentary

40″   barrage of images: • A self-inflicted   "death by a thousand   cuts."

    • A god who out of uncontrollable   anger devours   himself until there are only   his eyes

50″   and ravenous mouth left.   • LaMichael   making

breakfast of himself   one   finger   at a time.

0"

10"   In the fall

of 1989,   I mentioned   to Virgil Thomson   that I was going   to spend   New

20"   Year's   in   Venice,   my   first   visit

there.   He said,   "Venice,

30"

40"

50"

it's   wonderful,   but you must never go alone.   It's too tragic..."

0″

Rockland Lake is overpopulated with Canadian

Geese.

10″

The problem became acute some years back, with so many complaints about the

20″

aggressiveness of the birds and their filth that the authorities decided to take drastic action and, under

cover of darkness, killed many of them. Some in the community were so appalled that they compared this

30″

clandestine action to exterminations committed by the Nazis.

Processing the meat, grinding

40″

it up into goose-burgers with the intention of feeding these

to the homeless, the authorities tried to put the best

50″

spin on it. Unfortunately,

the meat was inedible as it was gravely tainted with PCBs...

0″ { On the mesa, in the

Casita, writing a lecture, tending the fire, watching the first sunset

10″ { of 2012, reading a book of John Cage's writings, attempting

a story about the failing light while carrying on a text-message exchange

20″ { with my nephew Avanni. It is nerve-racking, exciting, and completely

indeterminate.

30″ {

One thing is missing: an organizing system, like time limits to each activity.

40″ {

I could have used

50″ { a clock, but made do

with the sun- set .

94

0″ { Anna — or was it Estella? — told the story of a young male relative in the South living on a remote farm back in the days when young boys had to wear short }

10″ { pants. As the story goes, he was sitting on a fence, looking down the road that ran past his family's farm, when his mother said, "Hey, today is your birthday and you're a }

20″ { man!" }

30″ { }

40″ { Without so much as a word to anyone, }

50″ { he went into the house, changed from short pants to long ones, and left — never to be heard from again! }

0″ It was the fall of 1974 in Binghamton. I moved in a fog of guilt and uncertainty,

convinced that the only reliable life for me would be monastic. I was practicing yoga and

10″ chanting Hare Krishna daily. A guru had to be the solution: after all, "When the student is

ready the teacher appears." Alone down on my knees, performing my

20″ job at the university library, a voice said, "I have been looking for you!" I looked up into

the face of a handsome East Indian man beaming down at me. I was thunderstruck!

30″ Actually, he had been looking for a space to conduct his meditation

classes and someone must have told him I was a member of a dance collective with a loft in

40″ downtown Binghamton. I became one of his students, a vegetarian, and proposed celibacy to

Arnie. One Saturday morning at a street fair I bumped into Mirza, my teacher, eating a hot dog and

50″ strolling with his wife. I was shaken, though nothing was said then or later. He did teach me a number

of mind-focusing exercises. We saw less and less of one another, and then he moved away.

50

0" { Max Roach told of the day when Abbey Lincoln and he were

10" { excitedly putting the finishing touches on a Thelonious Monk tune

to which Abbey

20" { had written lyrics.

30" { They were excited because Monk himself

was to come by. He came,

40" { listened intently to their performance, whispered something into

Abbey's ear, and then left. Max asked her what Monk had said.

50" { And here Max, doing a perfect imitation of Monk's curiously

gruff, gravelly speech, whispered, "Next time, make a mistake!"

0″

My sister Rhodessa tells me that on the morning after my father had died of a heart attack

10″

members of the family were gathered at my mother's apartment. Estella, always

emotional, was completely transported by her grief. Weeping, shouting, sometimes

20″

praying, she went through ever-mounting peaks of emotion. Her San Francisco

railroad apartment — a series of rooms connected by a long hallway — resounded with her agony.

30″

Estella, at two hundred pounds, crashed about her living room, kicking

and screaming like a child, pushing away anyone who tried to comfort her.

40″

At one moment,

50″

howling, she threw herself on the floor and proceeded to roll from one end of the hallway

to the other as a child would on a grassy hillside in the springtime.

52

0″

story:

I've always enjoyed this

10″

20″

John Aubrey reports in his *Brief Lives* that Edward de Vere,

Earl of Oxford, acutely embarrassed at breaking wind in the presence of the Queen,

30″ had imposed upon himself seven years of exile.

40″

On his return she said:

50″

"My Lord, we had forgot the fart!"

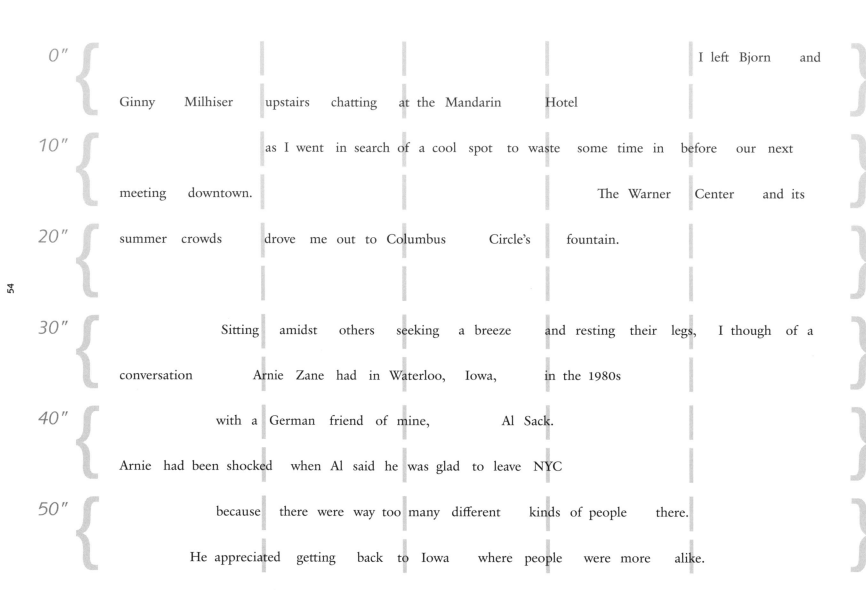

0″ { I left Bjorn and

Ginny Milhiser upstairs chatting at the Mandarin Hotel

10″ { as I went in search of a cool spot to waste some time in before our next

meeting downtown. The Warner Center and its

20″ { summer crowds drove me out to Columbus Circle's fountain.

30″ { Sitting amidst others seeking a breeze and resting their legs, I though of a

conversation Arnie Zane had in Waterloo, Iowa, in the 1980s

40″ { with a German friend of mine, Al Sack.

Arnie had been shocked when Al said he was glad to leave NYC

50″ { because there were way too many different kinds of people there.

He appreciated getting back to Iowa where people were more alike.

129

0″   "Two Bears"   by Hafiz

Once, after a hard day's forage,   two bears sat together in

10″   silence   on a beautiful vista,   watching the sun go down

and feeling deeply grateful   for life.

20″   Though, after a while, a thought- provoking conversation began,

which turned to the topic of fame.   The one Bear said,   "Did

30″   you hear about Rustam?   He has become famous and travels from city to city in a golden

cage;   He performs to hundreds of people

40″

who laugh and applaud

50″   his carnival stunts."   The other Bear thought for a few

seconds, then started weeping.

21A

0″ { Dora Amelan tells wonderful stories about her life. She is 90 years old, but re-

members many details from her younger years. When she is enjoying a good meal, she will sometimes

10″ { quote her father, Karl, who must have been quite witty with an ironic sense of humor who —

when asked how he was enjoying a delicious meal — would quip: "There is better, but it is more

20″ { expensive." I had recently worked restaging a show at the National Theatre in London.

My production supervisor was a delightful, warm, and very capable woman called Tanya.

30″ { The opening night was triumphant. At the party afterward we were all standing together

having a drink when someone asked how I had found working with her. I was very happy

40″ { with her and the whole experience at the National, so happy in fact that I decided

I too would be ironic and humorous. "There is better, but it is more expensive," I said.

50″ { I could see she was shocked. I tried to explain, but it was too late.

"You're not an old Jewish man," she said. "Just say something nice next time!"

0" I knew the monologist Spalding Gray casually in the 1980s. He and Renée

Shafransky, a woman I had known from the Cinema Department at SUNY Binghampton

10" in the 1970s, were a couple for a while and we went out for dinner together once.

All I remember of the evening is walking across Prince Street,

20"

30"

40" between West Broadway and Thompson Street,

talking about memory. I asked Spalding if he had read Proust, who demonstrated

50" something profound about memory in his great novel. He didn't seem very

interested. Dropping his eyes and his voice he muttered, "No, I haven't!"

0"

Small boys thinking: Dariki —

10"

about seven years old —

had left everyone else

20"

and sat alone on his great-grandmother Estella's bed,

very quietly,

30"

doing nothing — or so I thought as I came into the room.

40"

He felt me looking at him, turned, and said, "There must be

about a million things."

50"

I said, "Where?" He answered,

"You know, everywhere."

0"

10"

20"

30"

40"

50"

After braving sleet, snow, and ice we finally reached a diagnostic clinic on lower Second Avenue for a routine medical procedure that required anesthesia, or "a really lovely sleep," as the anesthesiologist described it. I was taken to examination bay number six, a simple bed with a curtain on a track that the nurse pulled closed while instructing me to undress, put on a gown, and wait. All of the staff were cheerful and polite. As the only partitions were drawn brown curtains, the various conversations filling the air were actually heightened as I lay obediently in my hospital gown under a warm blanket. My nurse asked if I had a medical power of attorney document or a DNR (DO NOT RESUSCITATE). I told her I did not, to which she gently responded: "In the future though, you should have such a document and carry it with you. It does not really matter here, today, because if something should go wrong we will do everything possible to revive you no matter what!"

0" { Just as I was settling into my assignment of writing down John Cage's report of an answer Jasper

Johns was giving to a Swiss journalist, my sister Flo called. We seldom see each other and

10" { never speak on the telephone. Recently we had seen each other in Washington. She and

my sisters Rhodessa and Johari were my guests in a weekend of celebrations. It was not a re-

20" { laxed phone call and we had both been nervous about speaking, as there had been an unpleasant

occurrence just before we were allowed into the White House. Still, a lot of words were ex-

30" { changed. Flo has a telephone manner that distrusts silences, so it was difficult to establish a conversa-

tional rhythm of give and take. We never did talk about what happened, but instead re-

40" { counted our shared memories of the famous, glamorous people, their jewelry, and the barrage of

impressions that she said had exhausted her and me too, I suppose. Nothing was directly addressed

50" { and nothing was revealed, but we did talk. We did laugh. We did remember.

After I hung up, there was that still space I felt whenever I stopped the John Cage recording.

0″ { We had just seen *Bill Cunningham New York*, a documentary about the New York Times photographer. He is an interesting character, very much of the old gen-

10″ { teel world. So much so that when asked if he were gay he answered that his family never spoke of such things and, as a result, he'd never given it much thought either.

20″ { He is a man in his 80s, a solid bridge to another time, like Merce Cunningham who is now gone.

30″ {

Leaving the film and passing the Joyce Theatre, we saw

40″ { that Merce Cunningham's company would be doing one of its last seasons there. It was a Monday night, the marquee was not lit.

50″ {

It was sobering seeing Merce's name as night was falling on a darkened marquee.

0" { As I lay in bed, left hand gone numb holding the iPad, right hand pecking at the keyboard, trying to start another story — a story about something that happened almost 40 years ago —

10" { an uncanny thing happened, commonplace yet strange. I lay on my back and through a corona of mist a perfectly round moon revealed itself. I thought that saying

20" { "The moon revealed itself to me" was like a pool of water laying claim to the ring

30" { of light that plays on its surface. In some seasons the full moon glares in the middle of the night, but that night and at that moment, the mist and the moon itself were gentle

40" { and personal.

However, the time spent struggling

50" { with typing, poor spelling, and a small thought barely able to tug along a big feeling was too much for the moon. It was still there when I turned away from the screen, but it was no longer mine.

0"

10"

20"

At a luncheon   one day in Washington   I sat next to Geoffrey

30"

Holder.   At one point I asked him his opinion   on my choice for a new stage work based on *Super Fly*,

the movie.   He said, "Marvelous!"   I asked him what he thought people

40"

would think about me making a work based on what they might think was an exploitation   of Black culture

and Black people.

50"

He mouthed   the words: "Fuck   them"

160

0" During a studio visit at Skowhegan an artist
showed me childhood pictures of himself and his family in which — with a Magic Marker —

10"

20"
he had crudely scribbled himself out so what one saw

30" were groups of smiling people, most often looking at the camera, and in their
midst a shadow... I asked him if he were angry.

40"
I can no longer remember what

50"
he said.

64

0″

When I last saw Estella in the hospital bed she barely recognized me, and yet when they placed one of her great-grandbabies on her chest and the little one started rooting around,

10″

grunting with pleasure, pulling at her nightgown and cheeks, sucking on her chin, her eyes opened and she smiled. Estella wanted nothing more than to stand up, but the best

20″

she could do was to sit in a specially constructed chair, placed there by nurses and a "lift team."

30″

Barely able to speak, she wanted to sing, and she sang the same song, over

40″

and over.

Walk with me, Lord. Walk with me.
Walk with me, Lord. Walk with me.
While I'm on this tedious journey
Walk with me, Lord. Walk with me.

0" Harris, my oldest brother, told me this story:

One day in the 1930s when he was a small boy in the South — Estella's first of twelve children — he

10" was with his mother and her best friend as they finished picking the cotton in one field and had to walk a

considerable distance to another.

20" A car with two white men in the front seat offered them a lift.

Reluctantly the two young women and the three-year-old Harris got into the back seat.

30" The two men, talking and laughing with each other, began to casually

reach back and grope between the women's legs or feel their breasts.

40"

I can't remember why he told me this story so many years later, but I do

50" remember the strained look of distaste on his face as he recounted how both women were silently weeping,

weeping, shuttling the boy between them as protection from the men's hands.

0″ { Another story my mother told — I'm not sure if she witnessed it or if she was recalling her mother

Anna's memory. Here too there is a small child, three years old or so, much loved

10″ { and curious to a fault. It seems that the family was living in a small shack or was

it a rundown tenement somewhere in the South and the children were often left alone.

20″ { The apartment was infested with rats, and rat poison was placed in holes in the walls.

Was it its shape, its color, its smell?

30″ {

40″ {

50″ { For whatever reason this small child was fascinated with it. She

was found "stiff as a board, standing dead on tiptoe with her face in the wall," my mother said.

0″

Wooster Street at Houston — the last day of spring.

10″ Indulging in a bit of racial looking, I noted how Soho had so many more

young Black men and women walking in the streets.

20″ The police had put up barriers at the intersection, behind which many of these

young people in sagging jeans, t-shirts, baseball caps, sneakers, and backpacks

30″ were surging in anticipation… Of what?

I reached down into my bag for a pen and sat back up

40″ just as the crowd broke through the barriers into Houston Street's traffic

in pursuit of a black SUV in which we could see

50″ a laughing Black face and an extended arm stretched out of the back window

videotaping the shrieking crowd's futile attempt to overtake it.

125

0″ The chances of hailing a cab seemed slim on 9th Avenue and 43rd Street. The heat, wall of buses and taxi cabs changing shift,

10″ not to mention the crowd of people on the streets and at every intersection, made it difficult to move, much less be noticed standing in the gutter, signaling.

20″ I walked a bit farther down to 42nd Street and, trudging across the intersection, saw a large woman in a pair of ill-fitting shorts bending forward. She was brown-

30″ skinned with a remarkably ruined body and a face to match.

40″

She was looking back over her backside and saying with terrible verve

50″ and a bitter humor to someone in the crowd, "You know what you can do with that, don't you? You can stick it right in here!" as she pointed to her ass...

69

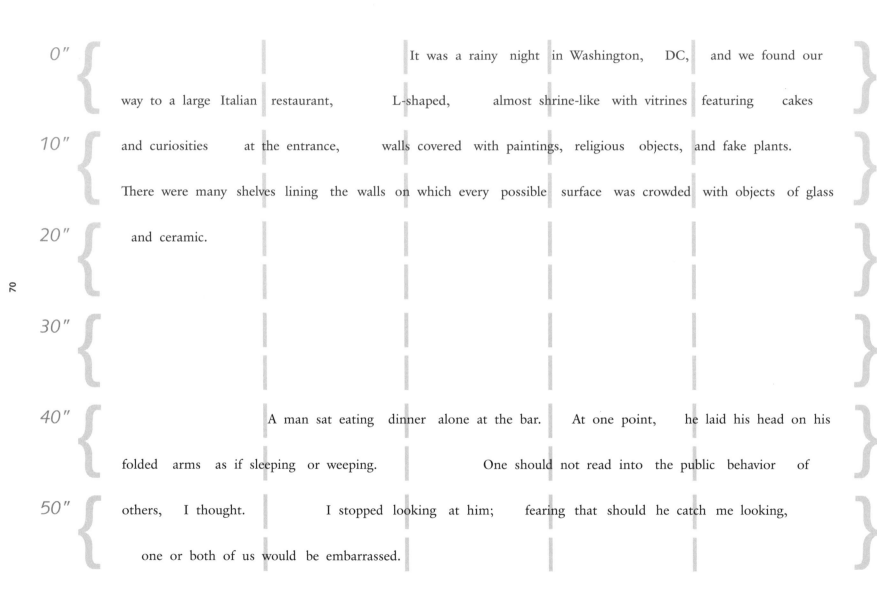

0″ { It was a rainy night in Washington, DC, and we found our

way to a large Italian restaurant, L-shaped, almost shrine-like with vitrines featuring cakes

10″ { and curiosities at the entrance, walls covered with paintings, religious objects, and fake plants.

There were many shelves lining the walls on which every possible surface was crowded with objects of glass

20″ { and ceramic.

30″ {

40″ { A man sat eating dinner alone at the bar. At one point, he laid his head on his

folded arms as if sleeping or weeping. One should not read into the public behavior of

50″ { others, I thought. I stopped looking at him; fearing that should he catch me looking,

one or both of us would be embarrassed.

42

0"

10"

20"

It was the summer of 1981   or so and I

30"   was performing   a solo on a makeshift   stage   as part of a daylong arts festival   in Milwaukee.

My friend Renata Sack had driven from Waterloo, Iowa,   to see me and join her good friend Ruth Gau,

40"   just recently   returned from China.   That afternoon   I went shopping   with the two of them in a vast

vintage clothing warehouse.   At one point they were suggesting   shirts that would suit me.

50"   Ruth held to my chest a 50s-era shirt in red and gold,   asking how I liked it.   I said with some scorn,

"I'm not into nostalgia!"   She answered: "You will be."

0″ It was early March and the first truly spring-like day. I was setting

breakfast outside in the garden, listening to the radio as Brian Lehrer spoke with a politician about the

10″ efforts to dismantle Public Broadcasting. In my mind's ear, I could hear my dancer, LaMichael,

shouting in *Fondly Do We Hope . . . Fervently Do We Pray*, "I'll be perfectly free, Goddammit!"

20″ Suddenly in the

30″ morning sunshine, like two dancers taking the stage, a couple of robins spiraled upward in

glorious flight, mating in midair . . .

40″

50″

72

0"

10"

March 23, 2011,   5:50 p.m.

20"

I am composing   this story   driving north

30"

on 10th   Avenue.

Intermittently   throughout   the day

40"

I have been feeling   like crying   or breaking   something.

I wonder   if this story   is better

50"

if I don't explain

why.

0″

Thinking back to the first showing of *Story*

10″ /*Time* in Phoenix, Simon Dove

had complained that he could not understand the structure as — in a work so dependent

20″ on one-minute increments — events and stories sometimes ended early or late.

30″

Later he said to me, "I hope I don't have

40″ to explain myself." I answered: "No."

50″ However, later

that day and for weeks, I thought, "Yes! Hell yes…"

0″ Tiny Mo was my grandmother's cousin. Perhaps she was not even related, but this detail is lost as all of the players

10″ are long since dead. Tiny Mo was a much beloved child who through her considerable charm and beauty affected all who came in contact with her.

20″ As the story goes, she must have been about four or five years old when my grandmother, Anna Edwards, herself only 9 or 10 was visiting Tiny Mo and her family. Tiny

30″ Mo's father was pumping kerosene from a small tank into the stove one evening. Tiny Mo was entertaining all the other children when a freak accident occurred whereby the pump shot a jet of

40″ flaming fuel that set the child ablaze. She was fatally burnt, but did not die immediately. Wrapped in white

50″ cotton and fat, she held on for many days, calling my grandmother, whom she loved, by name, saying over and over: "Anna, Anna, my Daddy done burnt me up."

0″ { After all of Antonio's | years of experience | people were still telling him |

they think it's easy to settle down.   But they never thought | how

10″ { he thought.   Antonio could have a woman that he loves | and

that treated him right,   and that still would never stop him from having

20″ { double desserts in every town.   Tour was a wonderful thing. |

The adventure got him every time,   but that was the thrill of it for him.

30″ { Antonio was always ready to release himself at any moment |

with any woman. He   was   a   pro

40″ { at   it.   But he still wasn't satisfied, in fact he was lonely.

It didn't hit him until one day he remembered the great words of his wise

50″ { mother. She would always say,   "You have two heads to think with,   always trust the one with two

eyes not just the one.   Two eyes are always smarter than   one."

0"

10"

As Arnie set up his camera to photograph Louise Nevelson on the roof of the Stanhope Hotel in San

20"

Francisco in 1973 or '74, they chatted. Nevelson was in her late 50s, wearing

her signature floor-length paisley coat with chinchilla lining, a headscarf, three sets of false

30"

eyelashes, and a jockey's cap. "What do you do other than photos?" she asked. "I'm a

dancer," he said. "Fantastic! Every artist must dance. Now, shall we begin?"

40"

She hawked up a wad of phlegm, spat it out, and then, like a fashion model, pulled the fur

around her and stared directly into the camera's lens.

50"

0″

Walking in Singapore, looking for a massage.

10″
They all seemed the same though some offered a kind of ear-therapy wherein paper-thin

sheets of wax are melted into one's ear then carefully removed, ostensibly dragging impurities

20″
out. The young woman tending to me would or could not explain what I would

experience.

30″

40″
I lay there on my side in a state of alarm, as it seemed an impossible amount of hot wax was

being directed into my ear canal. Just when I thought I couldn't stand it any longer and without warning, she ripped

50″
it all out, refusing to show it to me. I had been unaware and uninterested in these impurities when they were inside

my body, but now — as they were outside — I was desperate to see them!

150

0" During a snowstorm, Cecil Taylor, Arnie Zane, and I stepped into the Blue Note,

shaking off the snow in the uncanny stillness of Sixth Avenue.

10" Cecil introduced us to an array of personalities, some well known, all lovers of

jazz, and Abbey Lincoln in particular who sat quietly at the bar in between sets.

20" This was the treat Cecil had promised us earlier that evening. We had met at the insistence

of Max Roach who envisaged a collaboration between Cecil, himself, and the two of us for the Brook-

30" lyn Academy of Music's brand-new Next Wave festival.

Meeting with Cecil he had quickly dismissed

40" Max as "that old bebop drummer" and passionately insisted we consider Abbey Lincoln instead as he was

more that intrigued by her style and "this thing she does, past words, past singing."

50" He kept repeating, "Man, it's a sound she makes. A sound…"

0"

10" Michel Auder was sharing his latest multi-monitor video diary work with a small group of friends. Each tiny screen was a nonstop collage of imagery culled from thirty years of looking

via a handheld video camera. Though the various screens did sometimes echo or comment on each

20" other, there was a great deal of chance, giving the entire work a scattered and ecstatic quality.

The viewer was required to glide above and scan individual

30" events, to abandon any attachment to particular images. This generated a sort

of vertigo when one resisted the flow.

40" Later, over dinner, I made an

awkward attempt to explain to Michel how his work had forced me to confront my own seeing / selection

50" process. Always brusque and humorous, he said,

"You motherfucker! You were thinking about yourself while watching my work!"

11:12

New ideas? The question is what are we going to do with the ones we've got!

> —Choreographer Daniel Nagrin in an address to his improvisational dance company, The Work Group

Still other seeds fell on good soil. It came up and yielded a crop, a hundred times more than was sown. When he saw this, he called out: "He who has ears to hear, let him hear."

> —Luke 8:8

If you don't underestimate me, I won't underestimate you!

> —Bob Dylan

Let us look forward by first looking back. John Cage's take on the life of the artwork—in his case the musical composition—has three separate elements:

1. The compositional experience and its demands on the maker.
2. The experience and demands of its execution or performance.
3. The experience of the auditors/spectators/audience.

For Cage these were three entirely distinct experiences. I find this position both a comfort and a provocation. I do not, however, embrace it as my own. Why is this?

An artist, through his or her form, language, and structure, builds a bridge from his/her inner world to the outside world.

Which outside world? While I would like to agree with Cage that the essential criteria for a valid work is that it must reveal something "new" for the artist first, and only then for the public, I cannot. There has been a paradigm shift in society that affects the question of what this relationship is to the audience.

I have said it on more occasions than I can remember, but it's worth repeating once again:

I am often asked what should an artist do. I say an artist does not have to do a goddam thing. Artists should be the freest in our society, running—sometimes literally—naked through the world, thumbing their nose at any dogma or received wisdom. However, the artist is a person with a gender, a race, an ethnicity, an economic/educational location—a class, and a history. What does that person who the artist is need to do?

I have always wanted to be part of a larger conversation. And to see more people, such as the people I come from—people of color, poor people, people not typically defined as art consumers or an intellectual elite—in my audience. What must I change or adjust to invite them in? I have given permission to myself to use popular idioms, a broad spectrum of music, and, most importantly, to keep my dance company representative of a varied demographic.

In the final movement of *We Set Out Early . . . Visibility Was Poor* (1999), all the dancers are gathered together and instructed to move in a tight group on a diagonal, to exit. I asked them to dance in any way they would if at a party or a club. It was splendid to see the gyrations, the pumping of fists and arms, nodding of heads, roiling undulations, and activated pelvises riding a crescendo of finger snaps, hand claps, and party sounds. It was so easy to access and a relief for many of them, I think.

After the performance, Saundra Robinson, my niece, very excited, said: "*Uncle Bill, I'll be honest with you—I don't usually understand your dances, but that part, I could really feel.*" This comment remains one of my favorites ever offered about my work. Why did Saundra's comment please me? She was a rare viewer of my work: young, working-class, Black, representing a new generation of the Black community in general and my family in particular. She was actually present and embracing something I had made, declaring she could literally feel it! It had given her pleasure. She represented a community I had—justifiably or not—felt estranged from.

Why?

Because the type of work I have engaged in and generated since the beginning of my career demanded I leave this community. (Or did it leave me?) I had accepted the art historical narrative that said that a significant work must by its very nature be suspect to the majority of people, as only the few can "crack the code" of a new art form with the unique language of its unique maker. Gradually I came to have my doubts . . .

Recently we performed Fondly Do We Hope . . . Fervently Do We Pray *at the Kennedy Center in Washington, DC. The work uses many elements. We have toiled relentlessly in order to fashion a seamless whole. In the first night's postperformance discussion, a man stood up and asked what has never changed in my work over the years. "Doubt," I said, "It burns like fire."*

As Artistic Director of the recently formed New York Live Arts, a reimagining of the historic and innovative Dance Theater Workshop (DTW) and of the Bill T. Jones/Arnie Zane Dance Company, I am privileged to see much ambitious work self-described as "progressive" and outside the mainstream. I am often struck by how little these works seem to take the audience into their consideration other than through a knowing nod and a wink to the in-crowd, the "community," what Steve Paxton described as "the research branch of the field." Here Cage's concept seems almost a reflex and a posture. Still, this desire to play to one's constituency cuts in more than one way. Even as I might criticize Cage for his part in an insider culture, I realize in trying to return home to some racial/social identification as a Black man that I too rely on a "gated community" view of certain cultural practices—jazz, for instance.

I suppose my niece Saundra's approval reminded me of my loneliness and disorientation. It was as though I was an immigrant who hears a snatch of song or tastes a food that reminds him of "the old country." It makes him wonder if he can ever go home while recalling all the complex reasons that caused him to leave.

People say you can never go home again. I say—for most of us—we can never leave home as we carry it around with us while striving to be free of it.

Maya Angelou

Starting out as a dancer, and it's essential that I add, young male dancer, I was overtaken with the discovery of the strength in my young body, its appetite for space, and its reveling in its own image. I sometimes describe this as wanting to feel and be "fabulous." But with the passage of time and after learning more about what I did not know about the act of dancing and about the art form itself, I realized that I had waded into a tradition that seemed to stretch endlessly behind me and in front of me. For better or worse, I began a conversation with this tradition. All those hours dancing in the light of the jukebox or in front of the stereo amounted to nothing—or so I had come to think. Dance as art had come into my life. In other words: at first, dance was simply a way of being, and then making dance, making art, became a language and a mode of understanding the world and my place in it—a negotiation with the world, and perhaps even a weapon against it.

This coming into consciousness had other streams as well. There has also been—and for me, it is a reality as true as gravity—a desire for transcendence.

The notion of transcending the world is fraught with a set of psychological and emotional impulses. To transcend implies there is something one wants to get rid of, to get away from. This was certainly the idea behind my foray into spirituality!

It was sundown in the summer of 1972, and Arnie Zane and I were standing, hitchhiking on the New York State Thruway trying to get a ride home to Brockport from Buffalo. The State Troopers had already threatened arrest if they caught us standing where we were. We had retreated up the ramp, but decided to risk going back, as night was falling.

For the week prior, we had been at New Brindavan, the Krishna Consciousness retreat, in West Virginia, chanting and praying from before dawn to late into the night. The rhythmic clanging of cymbals, pounding of drums and ecstatic shouts of "Govinda Jiah! Jiah! Gopahla Jiah! Jiah!—Govinda Jiah! Jiah! Gopahla Jiah! Jiah!" was still ringing in my ears, mixed with the whoosh and roar of sixteen-wheelers, family cars, and buses.

We were very small, very high, and very alert as the stars came out.

With time the idea of transformation has become ever more compelling, by turns exhilarating and sublime in the sense of eliciting awe verging on terror. As a young dancer, there is delight taken as one sees one's body transform, as one acquires the skills of transforming what was on the athletic field a purely utilitarian leap over a hurdle or a pit of sand into a poetic, polished jeté, a metaphor for flying. Later, this acquired and embodied knowledge becomes attached to a vision of a self that could in an instant transform from human being to the idea of human being. So yes, I wanted transformation as well.

Transformation of the world?

Which category of the world did I want to transform? The part that joined my voice to the voices of people across the country and the globe crying out "We shall overcome" in the age-old communal cry for social justice?

Or the part of transformation that turns one into a free person, a powerful person, a desirable person—who says: "I am not what the world tells me I am. I can adopt a lifestyle, choose friends, in a way that transforms me into a vision of myself more in keeping with a imagined world in which I am in control"?

John Cage's notion of art making as self-alteration, of *disappearing* in the work and becoming a vessel for transformation, held an exquisite attraction for the young self faced with these choices.

Why keep connecting him with his work? Don't you see that he's a human being whereas his work isn't? If for instance you decided to kick his work and him, you would wouldn't you have to perform two actions rather than a single one. The more he leaves his work the more useable it becomes . . . Room in it for others.

John Cage, *Diary: How to Improve the World (You Will Only Make Matters Worse)*

At the same time, I remain conflicted about Cage. Who was he speaking to? Whom was he making his work for? Was there room for someone like me in his milieu?

I imagine that he would respond, "He who has ears to hear, let him hear! I don't care what color they are." I would be obliged to respond, in turn, "But John, that might be enough for you, but it's not enough for me!" What would be enough? I don't know yet . . .

I have a hot core of indignation and identification that says that art comes from a certain experience. I prize that experience. And yet I don't want to be oppressed by my experience.

Philip Bither, the Performance Curator at the Walker Arts Center, once told me that when he asks young jazz artists "Well, what is jazz?" many of them don't want to call it jazz anymore. They want to call it contemporary improvisational music. So maybe they don't care anymore about "guarding the sacred hot core of the Black experience."

Art making, for me, is participation in the world of ideas. Cage had a very powerful idea. Now I would like to say that he is an ally in my struggle for truth, honesty, freedom—all those things that have come very much from my position as a Black man born in the mid-twentieth century. That Cage's aesthetic, abstracted worldview extends the project of social justice. So I have no intention of making Cage into simply an old white guy.

I've said repeatedly that Cage's ideas are a kind of a comfort and a provocation. The comfort is a sense that here was a man who was shockingly disconnected from the world and who had found a very high-minded system of investigation that involved removing one from one's tastes, preferences, and feelings in order to create something new and unforeseen out of chance operations. That's the big one for me. Did he really want to be free of his feelings?

What is art? Isn't art—the experience of art making, the execution or performance of art—about feelings? Cage claimed that feelings are a trap—we're always going to go to the feelings we know and avoid the ones we don't like.

My point is not that Cage's philosophy of non-intention is wrong. But there is another way to make art in which art is indeed about feelings, taste—and intention.

Cage encourages us to "get out of the way and experience the joy." I suspect his "willed bonhomie" coexists with if not masks a great deal of frustration and anger. He insists that the goal of the composer/creator is to find something new. I suspect he was "settling scores" as well.

After some forty years in the art world and among artists, I have come to believe that most artists have a beleaguered sense of their place in a profane and mediocre world. Cage—and other important artistic leaders like himself—in their lack of concern for audience, have led several generations of creators to adopt a worldview that is, quite simply, an attitude—an attitude of distance and remove:

> **They taught us art was self-expression—you had to have something to say. They were wrong. You don't have to say anything. Think of the others as artists. . . . Art is self-alteration.**
>
> John Cage, *Diary: How to Improve the World (You Will Only Make Matters Worse)*

With time our discourse about the place of the artist in the world—particularly in the world of movement-based art—has gone through paroxysms of euphoria and despair. At this moment the discourse has sunk into grim utilitarianism. I recall a meeting with a major funder on the subject of arts funding for education during which we were told that many traditional funders were now evermore interested in how the arts could help children achieve basic proficiency in reading and math.

Former Arizona State University educator Simon Dove puts forward a vision of educating artists that is related to both John Cage's ideas and my own, but with a pronounced pragmatism:

> **If only 6% of the population claim to attend dance performances, then that leaves a massive 94% who find no purpose in attending. Clearly current dance practice does not make sense to most people.**

If institutions are training dance artists so that their work can only be seen in expensive buildings with high specification floors, controlled temperatures, advanced technical facilities, and broad sightlines, then Western society is simply consolidating that separation. In the pursuit of the highest standards in dancing, it is important not to forget the critical importance of us knowing why we are dancing, for whom, and to what end.

How can professional dance activity be more relevant to more people?

These are central questions for any artist in the 21st century, and students who begin this process of self-inquiry whilst still at college are years ahead of those who only begin to engage with these questions when confronted by the realities of professional life.

What is their role and responsibility as an artist in the world today? How can they use their artistry, for example, to work meaningfully with a group of homeless young people? How can they use their movement knowledge to explore the stories of people who speak a different language? Confronting these questions opens the dance artist to imagining solutions that are not taught in the classroom, but where the cumulative skills, knowledge, and person-al understanding of the world are applied to achieve very tangible, practical, and creative solutions.

We need to foster a shift towards respecting and supporting the artist, not just the finished work; to invest in the artist's presence in our world, and not only the product. Our mission here at ASU is clear; we are becoming a training ground for socially engaged and innovative artists, who use dance as their primary means of engagement. A cultural practice based on products is not dynamic. A cultural landscape based on seeding artists to thrive in diverse contexts will evolve and give rise to work we cannot yet imagine, and transform people and society in ways we have only dreamed of.

This manifesto is curious and troubling as we consider the reach and legacy of Cage's third aspect of creation: the experience of the creator versus the audience. Dove is so concerned with audience that he would set out to train a generation of artists not to (as Cage would say) go out in search of what is new for them, but to find what is useful to a solving a social-political problem. I find this troubling, especially when I recognize how this talk echoes my own voice asking Cage to be more aware and responsive to me as an audience member. Troubling, and confusing: Dove would have artists address the question "Why make work?" with the answer that:

- it is necessary in order to get a fractured, alienated public to attend live performances;
- as a means to "Improve The World."

I sense something of "social uplift" in his strategy. To be sure, it is a social uplift promising new forms, greater participation, and a greater symbiosis between creators and an uninvested public. I am a child of the 1960s—an era of good works such as the VISTA program and the Peace Corps. These programs sent armies of youthful volunteers nationally and internationally into backwaters (such as the one I grew up in) with the mission of helping the poor by building, teaching, uplifting cultural horizons, and, ultimately, providing a young, college-educated elite with a sense of connectedness to the otherwise undernourished and disenfranchised. I recognize what Simon Dove is saying all too well. His vision represents an enduring challenge to Cage's notion of artistic freedom as a way of changing the world.

Neither prescription—Cage's nor Simon Dove's—is satisfying to me. While I concede that both of them may create new forms or meanings, the world itself will remain unchanged.

As I bring this book to a close, feel free to hum under your breath your personal anthem of salvation—"We Shall Overcome," for instance—and forgive me if my wry tone jars or is dissonant in any way. With time this is where the discourse has left me. In the first part of this book, I evoked my younger self first exposed to Cage as a young man in the waiting room of the cultural discourse. Let's end by listening in on a conversation I had with Laura Kuhn about an old master who gave his life to a vision of transformation and self-alteration:

Laura Kuhn: Cage was quite ignorant about the world. He didn't wear a watch, he didn't read the newspaper. He didn't know that Jesse Jackson was Black. Really! When he found out about crack babies, he wept.

BTJ: Wow!

Laura Kuhn: I said, "How can you not have known about this?" and he said, "Oh, I don't know." You know? He had read something in a newspaper when he was working on his Harvard lectures. I had to come to terms with that very early on in my relationship with him, but he was really very cut off from the world. He was cut off from the grittiness of the world.

BTJ: Right, and I think that's almost the position of a cleric. People tried to do that with John, to make him a monk.

Laura Kuhn: God knows, he wasn't. He did have clerical leanings as a kid. The ministry was his first thought for an occupation.

BTJ: And it seems that he had a great fervor in his desire for, do I dare call it, transcendence? He wouldn't call it transcendence, being a Buddhist, but he definitely wanted to get to some sort of base principle of being.

Laura Kuhn: Yes, I think that's true.

BTJ: What would he say? Would he say transcend or transform?

Laura Kuhn: Well, I don't think he would have said either. If you look at his diaries, the recorded diaries, the title is, How to Improve the World (You Will Only Make Matters Worse).

BTJ: Yes, I love that title.

Laura Kuhn: Yes, and he really meant that. It's like you move with the way the world moves. You don't try to fix things. You don't try to change things. You just do. All you have control over is your own self-alteration.

. . .

BTJ: John Cage never wanted to be rich or powerful.

Laura Kuhn: Not at all. I can tell you a very interesting little fact with regard to being rich. There are so many instances that you can see in correspondences where he is beyond consoling over the fact that his mother is in a nursing home and he doesn't know where he is going to get the money to pay for that and Elaine de Kooning giving him $20 in a cab. Really, he had nothing. In 1987, he gave away more money than he had ever made in a previous year.

BTJ: Really?

Laura Kuhn: Yes, he was constantly giving people money, constantly. He had really no interest in being rich. He spent more money on flowers for his apartment than he did on anything else in his life. He would buy huge dogwood branches for the apartment.

BTJ: That was one of the things worth doing in life, which was enjoying beauty?

Laura Kuhn: I don't know. That's a surmise, but I don't know. All I can tell you is that he had hundreds of cacti and succulents and trees, and then he would adorn those with fresh flowers. He would send me to the flower market two or three times a week with $100 to come back with tulips. He wanted color. One time he laughed and said that he wanted the apartment to look like Bolivia.

BTJ: Bolivia?

Laura Kuhn: He said, "I like to think that they're not interested in modern music there." He dreamed of having a life where he wasn't constantly being called on to do transformative things, be the transformative character that he was, to live someplace with plants and bancha tea and chess and good red wine. So, those are all things that are palliative, pleasurable, of the senses.

In recent decades, in the era of identity politics, artists have had to be careful in their public declarations of which artists or thinkers have influenced them. Women artists, for example, often feel compelled in their communities to list other women artists when asked about their influences. To mention a male artist role model would be suspect. I am not immune from this cultural climate and have experienced similar anxiety in choosing to engage seriously with such a socially "unengaged" artist who seems to hark back to an era when the only artists who mattered where male and white. And yet engage with John Cage I must.

If one were to examine what I would call the DNA of one's influences, and see it in terms of how the various strands interact to create the artist, one would see how important conflict between the strands is. I don't think any artist can come to who they are without experiencing this conflict or perhaps without getting close to certain suspect influences. In some cases, one has to accept an uncomfortable fit in order to become the artist one truly is.

Betty Freeman was a great friend to contemporary music and a friend of mine. I met her at Bill Katz's loft the same night I met John Cage. She sat next to Cage at the far end of a long table, between him and Jasper Johns. As Arnie and I entered the room, she asked Bill, "Who is that? He's a dancer, right?"

Bill sat me near her and John. At one point she asked Cage to tell a story. As he began speaking she interrupted, saying, "Not that one, John. The other one."

Now, after thirty years, I can't remember either story . . .

Bill T. Jones is an artist, choreographer, dancer, theater director and writer. Mr. Jones began his dance training at the State University of New York at Binghamton (SUNY), where he studied classical ballet and modern dance. In 1982 he formed the Bill T. Jones / Arnie Zane Dance Company (then called Bill T. Jones/ Arnie Zane & Company) with his late partner, Arnie Zane. Currently he is Artistic Director and Choreographer of the Bill T. Jones / Arnie Zane Dance Company and Executive Artistic Director of New York Live Arts, a multi-disciplinary performance venue that serves as a resource for artists and a platform for the creation of new works and advocacy for contemporary performance. He is the recipient of many awards and honors, including the 2010 Kennedy Center Honors, the 2010 Jacob's Pillow Dance Award, a 2010 Tony Award for Best Choreography of the critically acclaimed *FELA!*, a 2007 Tony Award for *Spring Awakening*, a 2007 Obie Award for *Spring Awakening's* off-Broadway run, the 2005 Samuel H. Scripps American Dance Festival Award for Lifetime Achievement, the 2005 Harlem Renaissance Award, the 2003 Dorothy and Lillian Gish Prize, and a MacArthur "Genius" Award (1994). In 2010, Mr. Jones was recognized as Officier dans l'Ordre des Arts et des Lettres by the French government, and in 2000, The Dance Heritage Coalition named Mr. Jones "An Irreplaceable Dance Treasure."